RESCUE MISSION

RESCUE MISSION

Poems by
Gad Kaynar-Kissinger

Translated from Hebrew by Natalie Fainstein

atmosphere press

For Or, Noam and Matan. My children. My bliss and blessing.

CONTENTS

Freedom. A manifesto.

Do the right thing. Don't be tempted by the charms of obligation.

No man is obliged to oblige. So said Lessing, of all people, a man

Of the Enlightenment who taught us life itself is not enough, that one must

Conquer the heart's desire, to enslave oneself to the Moloch of obligation, to

Pierce our ear to its doorstep, to account rather than count the laughter of

Children aimed at us, to cordially ignore the flowers blushing at us,

To keep the books on the do, conclude, beware of the border head,

Of the firing squad on the other end of the deadline, control the herds

Of your actions on your schedule so that no bellwether stops to stare

And dream, don't step out to your yard at midnight to howl with the jackals,

Don't get carried away, God forbid, and burn your place down and with it all

Your inheritance, your heirs, your self, to rejoice like Nero in front of the

Flames,

And recite poetry.

The range of our voice is enormous, so once told me a vocal coach

Whose facial wrinkles, to me, were like the war paint of the Navajo Tribe,

And in his voice echoed the buffalo drums and the stampede of the beastly

Herd.

We use only one tenth of it, too anxious to break through

The corral fence, too scared to scare and to be scared and to plummet down

The breathtaking abyss that will gape inside us.

Therefore, do the right thing —

Scream, wake up the neighbors, curse wisdom, go on staycation.

Don't take anything with you, not even the clothes on your back,

Remove your skin from off your bones, fear not to penetrate

The throat of an active volcano, trap yourself a venomous viper for

A pet, and let it slither down the parlors of your brain, let your children out
Naked, don't mold them into bronze statues of ancient
Greek athletes, melt them, let them trickle like lava
That would cover and warm and decimate you. Go to an all-out war
Against obligation, destroy memos, notes, electric sheets,
Reminders on the fridge, get bitten more than once and don't ever be shy,
Sleep with the first person to exit your threshold, make love
To the door, the doorstep, the keyhole, the wound, the electric
Sockets and crowns, char yourself, write with the char chalk of your body
No no, and no and no and no, and again no. Honor thy father and thy mother
With a broom and dustpan, honor the dust, honor the raging virus,
Honor the whiteness of your hair, your dentures and spectacles, hold
A one-man demonstration for your advanced age, summon the angel of death
To your home, he is so tired, in dire need of rest, go with him,
Support him, pluck out his eyes, ascend with him to the cliffs of Dover,
Convince him to jump, but make sure he doesn't crash.
You will eventually find out you need him still, that you
Can still smile at each other with mouths vacant of useless
Teeth, to join your bony hands
And walk together,
Like the first couple that has just discovered love.

Beauty. A Sonnet Sans One Line.

I fail to illustrate your beauty with my words

As a restorer of a masterpiece whose brush falters

When it must touch the unparalleled Virgin Mary

Devoured by time in the darkness of the piece

Or by the sun that pinks the sky

After it has long since set

Into its womb.

I fail to find the voice to whisper your beauty

Like my foot, so careful not to

Trample on a bed of withered leaves of such intoxicating

Color in the blackest darkest forest

Just before the

Woodcutter.

Plagiarism

Your earrings are the quotation marks

Opening and closing your beautiful face,

Which I quote in light exhalations

Without reference

Or

Carnal Knowledge

Relationships 23;73

Relationship 23

They were far away from me.

The scorching sun, glisteningly nude as a Yeshiva

Student gone astray, dipping in the heretics' sacred pool

In the town square, only halfway satisfied,

Melted their shimmering bodies together

As if they were dancing the dance of

Saint Parkinson.

They were far away from me.

If I wanted to capture them, just like saints,

Embraced and burnt they would have

Mounted the stake of glistening

Light and my camera would have stored them

Inside an urn of white.

A temple for a new religion of

Love.

They were far away from me

When they noticed me they tried to pluck pieces of clouds

To cover their shame and chase

Their voices, plucked from them and pinned upon

Cruel wreaths of thorns tumbling in the wind:

I love yours, and I yours,

Deeper, deeper, yes, yes,

It's good, so good, so beautiful.
So.

They were far away from me
But then the eye grew accustomed
And the sun pulverized into a plethora of light-stamps
Which she affixed upon their enveloped bodies
Like a mischievous child
To send to a land too far away.
Too impossible.
Of a love too great.

Relationship 73

His cracked lips flutter for a kiss
Over her shriveled cheek as if to see
Whether that old glue still is strong
Enough to seal the Issue Day envelope
Encasing their wedding day's
Gift.

*

She will never tire
Of buying a plethora of doors in the frosty wind
Pulling at the hem of her dress like her retarded
Son who lost his way home.
And wants a hug.

She will never cease
Planting doors
Erecting luxury apartments
With no walls
Upon the wandering
Sands.
Until she finds the
Keyhole
To fit the key
Dangling from her neck
Like a noose.

And that same kiss
That opened.

*

At the mobile light
Whose battery is dying
She reads his thoughts.
I should get new glasses
She thinks.

A Classical Portrait of my Sleeping Love

When you sleep

Clouds glide by your face

Lighting screens are pushed aside

As in a Baroque theater

That closed down then reopened

Just for me.

Seasons turn

Pullies Squeal

Rats sing

As sets of scenery change

From hot.

To cold.

To frozen.

And clusters of painters' apprentices of the Flemish

School are bewildered to discover

The remains of fallen lights

In the trenches of your wrinkles

When you sleep.

When you sleep

Ever snow-covered Alpine ridges

Grow tall and collapse

Upon the blanket covering your breasts.

And I, the skier, am lying in the trench

At the bottom

Bones crushed

And glowing

Another Love Song
For Shlomi M., a heretic believer

Like a Torah scribe etching the entire bible

On the shell of an egg

With my bitten nails I etch the scrolls

Of my love for you on the stem of my hollow

Heart

And my blood's bishops rush urgent and breathless

Down the tunnels of my clogging veins to deliver

A replica of its behest to the last of my dying

Cells.

The road is paved with love blood cells

Joyful and red and white

Helpless

Like blacked out balloons after a party

That amid capsized chairs

On shattered bottles

The last of its guests

Spit and abandoned it

Continues to hum

To hug

And to dance

Itself

Tallises

To the enlightened Rabbi A., who endeared tolerant tradition to me

Let's envelop ourselves in our weighty silence

You embracing me and I embracing

You two tallises wrapping a non-

Body in the shrouds of its dark secrets.

Impossible to tell the fair from the

Foul the impure from the pure fused

Together in fresh oil as an act

Of love in a mass grave

Photographs of Love Like Love

Photographs of love like love:

It's best in gray and white.

In low resolution

In dull colors

On matte paper. Not the glossy kind.

Not too sharp.

It injures. It hurts too much.

Fact: the Werthers love it.

So does Stefan Zweig and the rest

Of yesteryear's tuberculars.

In such a photo even a faded bloody cough

Seems like a burst of laughter.

Photographs of love like love:

In gray and white

In low resolution

In dull colors

Affected photos

Of brides and grooms

As if documenting preparations to take down

The trash and carry bags

Up to the seventh-floor heaven,

And fuzzy hunched backs of

Naked people in a Polish forest on the edge

Of a hole are seen through the sight of the shooter

Or the photographer as if inflaming

A bonfire in a youthful orgy

Or peeing to

Extinguish it.

The Dark Lady and her Choking Lover

And I failed to say what I should have

And it weighed on me like a rock on the bosom

Of a fetus whom a motherly mob

Taught to drown in a warm

Pool of placenta fluids.

And at times I almost said that today so

It shall be, but it never was,

Instead, it sat there like a feckless stone, if turned

Reveals a drowsy scorpion stretching

And stinging itself to make its

Hatred infernal, and

Rest eternal.

And I still failed to say what I should have,

Because the words that hurried out trampled over

Each other and clogged in my throat like the fishbone

Of a spectacular fish that rose from the depths

Of the placenta pool.

And only as I turned blue

You said what should be said:

My aristocrat.

You are beautiful in blue.

Come to me in blue.

I shall remember you blue.

And suddenly what should have been said
Need not be said.

Silence

Silence stood between us.

Stood.

Wouldn't sit.

Or drink.

Stood.

Until we sat

Face to face.

Not looking.

Not holding hands.

Sitting.

Silent.

The Final Word

A door slams shut behind you.

Sometimes it's a hand.

Sometimes it's the wind.

Sometimes you slam shut

And coil inside yourself.

One can understand "Go forth"

In different ways that would lead

To different ways.

At times as a promise.

At times exile.

At times – over there

Unto the land that I will show thee.

At times just "disappear"

Just get the hell outta here

And don't even leave a space

That remembers you

That would remind of you

The stench of your sweat

A stain on the sheet

A toothbrush whose hairs

Bow humbly like a treetop

Making love to the stormy

Imprint of your teeth

A glass of wine where you left

A sample of your blood

And me

Nothing but the scene of

Your crime of passion.

Me

Your fingertips

Me

Who lacks the courage

To call you back after

The slammed door has had

The final word.

Yellowing Love Letters

At night when the envious walls veil themselves
With darkness and above us their stretched wings rehearse divine
Destruction, our body rehearses the posture of our birth and death.
Tucked within itself like a desperate envelope flap lest out of us
The yellowing love letters we once wrote
To ourselves
Will slip.

Masturbating Songbirds

The ancient Pistachio is confined

to a straitjacket with straps of steel

So that her splitting stem doesn't come apart

And her heat is restrained.

With the rings of her sightless eyes

She lusts after the tender seedlings.

Her suckling babes.

Masturbating songbirds.

Now Rationing our Love

Now Rationing our Love

So and so more grueling expeditions

In the ravines of wrinkles

So and so more engraved

Embraces to note that we were

So and so more mouth to mouth

Resuscitating kisses

Now Rationing our Love

As they do a lifer

Raising a paper rose in his cell coloring

It in with his daughter's crayons

Sprinkling it with fragrances of perfumed

Shaving water.

A paper rose

That would wilt

If released

Belated Electrocution

In the narrow hallway

Like a polygraph

Their bodies brush

Briefly

On their exhausting journey

Toward sleep.

The skin of their love is sealed.

A trusty smuggler suitcase

That doesn't give away diamonds

Wrapped in feculent

Underpants.

Not tonight.

Not tomorrow either.

Perhaps yesterday.

But as their bodies brush

Briefly in the narrow agonized

Hallway

Such lightning strikes them

Such fear and trepidation

Fraught with their passion

That it electrifies

And turns them into ashes.

A monument for an unparalleled

Missed

Fortune.

Rescue Mission

Like a sound sensor

Attached to a slab of cement

Of a collapsed palace

To pick up the faint bleats

Of survivors

I concentrate my gaze at your pupils

To pick up distant echoes

Of our former love.

And my hand, wandering through your black tresses,

And through the dark channels of your furrows,

Advances with the delicate, watchful

Choreography of brain and heart

Surgeons lest other stories

Crash on top of us

And let our souls die

With the years

P.S. From the Literary Remains: Probably a Love Song

To Ahuva. Whom else.

If you won't be one day I shall lie in your bedside

in which you wander for forty years now I shall turn

my back on myself lest I see my face and die

I shall pull the blanket to my side my feet to my

belly to spare myself

to hide from myself

to dream your dreams in which I am not

If we won't be one day I shall wear your nighty draw my testicles

into my body and remember me watching you sleep. How beautiful

you are. How awfully beautiful. And who am I to climb your tree to

pluck your fruit back in the days in which we believed that being old

is a matter of character not of age and if this might perhaps befall us

we shall kill ourselves together and today we hardly talk about who

will buy milk and after all suicide must be carefully planned and who

has got the power to do it and you don't die anymore from

unpasteurized milk, but the hand's infantile instinct still gropes

for the breast and the frightened heart for the hand.

If one day you won't be you shall still be what you shall be. I will lie

in your beside as a spy looking for a resting place beyond the lines.

Then I shall shudder since then I shall know you without your body,

I shall understand that if I am in your side then you are not

in your side, and I am neither in mine, and there is none to say you,

and none to answer I I I

Here I am

My Lord

My Wife

Here I am

My Maker

Take me

Me too

IN THE LANGUAGE OF PAIN

To Mother. In Memoriam

In My Mother's Drawer

In My Mother's Drawer

I found aerial photos

That mapped me

Out

From afar.

From above.

Un-Touching.

In the language of pain

You're laced in your robe like a brittle yellowing

Scroll summarizing the history of your misery.

The chapters are meticulously laid out in the furrows

Of your brow. You were always calculated. Everything

Filed and erased. Every load-off.

Including me.

We sit across from each other like two

Worn out army generals about

To sign a historic peace treaty. On

Your shriveled cheek I seek the line

Where the deal will be sealed with my kiss

And try to decipher how to pronounce the word love

In the language of pain.

If at all.

The Plague Park

For my brother Doron. In common memory.

As is her custom in sun bathed days draped in a flattering

Towel made of the soft breeze that strayed

From the sea my late mother sat in the balcony Motzkin

Twenty-nine overlooking the park wringing her slim

Fingers, ambushing the world. But the world

Never went past her. The park was still

And alert like the set of A Midsummer

Night's Dream that will never play because all its actors

Died in the plague and yielded like a dream.

Sometimes the faint voices of standby actors who were finally

Given a chance were heard memorizing in vain lines that will never

Be uttered. Other times a kindergarten teacher would happen there with

Her children playing on the squeaky rides weeping for the players who

Play no more. Occasionally a hustling-bustling band of craftsmen

Who teased the benches and disrespected the old trees on the

Trunks of which they smashed their empty Corona

Bottles. They forced out the teacher and her pups,

Dismantled the set of rides, and measured

The park to turn it into a mass grave for victims

Of the plague. That's when my mother startled awake from her dream

As the summer night befell the park as if she had never

Left me like a dream with the troupe of actors

To other parks

And singing rides

SONGS ON THE DEATH
AND RESURRECTION
OF A CHILD

Reconstruction Dream

Dead butterflies pluck the arms of sewn-eyed children

In a sutured dream. The pins I used to prick

Them in my childhood turned them into voodoo dolls that curse

Me in old age. Dead angels and expert butterflies now

Reconstruct, with gentle brushes, the heavens for my entrance.

Everything's so very frail, I am fragile, fractured,

Feeble, the paint's still fresh. With UHU glue, snowy owl's

Glue, God plasters the cracks of my demise, but

With sewn-up children's

Drawn out arms

The butterflies

Charge to my death-bed. Don't touch, says the nurse,

Wait a while, the death is still fresh.

Daniel in the Paper Den

Please lower the volume of the radio

So I can listen to my thoughts.

Allay a while the volume of my musings

So I can listen to the receiver

And erase my thoughts.

Like a child eagerly toiling

To erase an error in his notebook

And the eraser is consumed and on the page

A gaping den appears where all that isn't said is said

And nothing else matters but

The boy who fell inside to wrestle

With the snakes, the spells and with toothless

Stallions. Therein sprouts

His death.

Making an Impression

Like a mischievous child

Pressing his hand in the concrete mold

To make an impression

And the concrete clings to him and doesn't

Let go like a child who wants to make

An impression and doesn't let go in his despair

Until he tears himself

From himself.

From his hand.

The Silence

    After Ingmar Bergman

She anoints the vagina with blood.

Sets out to make graceless love.

Like a merciful mother she deposits her child

Down the corridor of a hotel as empty as the fallopian

Tube of a surrogate.

There's no mother on the one end.

Air on the other.

And her false pregnancy child who shot her

With a toy gun

Grew old.

His real gun aims

For the vagina. Quavering

In his trembling hands.

And there's no mother on the one end.

Air on the other.

And outside they're still transporting a tank

To some war in a baby

Carriage.

Krakow

For Marlyn Vinig

Before the Holy Ark in the Holy Rama
Synagogue in Krakow eighty kilometers
From Auschwitz-Birkenau a German children's choir
Sings Stabat Mater in voices sweeter than
Honey.

There are many ways to pierce the heart
Of the merciful God, as an army encircling
A barricaded city, stabbing its back with
A sugary knife and shoving inside her womb a rocking
Horse nectar and delicacies in the delicate voice
Of a child to sweeten the bitterness of our death.

Boy Drawing the Face of God

For my grandchildren

Boy drawing the face of God.

Scared of seeing his face in the mirror or in the still

Surface of the lake he borrows the face

Of the ferocious Samurai in a Manga magazine.

In his small hand, not yet skilled with the pen

He lingers with the lines as to not

Digress from them like a warrior who knows

That though this valley is quiet beyond

The hill the vultures are already

Reveling.

Boy drawing the face of God.

The angel of God stands behind him

Meticulously tracing along the lines

The boy's innocent face.

And rests it over his face.

God drawing the face of a child.

FROM NONE TO NO ONE

They tell that once, on the eve of Yom Kippur – the Jewish Atonement Day – after the evening prayer, the holy Rabbi Baal Shem Tov heard someone heavily weeping in the empty, darkened synagogue. He looked around, and finally in some barely detectable corner, he found the Creator crouched in a nook, sobbing. "Why are you crying, my Lord?", asked the holy Baal Shem Tov, his memory be blessed. "I'm so tired, Rabbi," said the Almighty. "So tired".

A Chassidic story. Presumably.

Go to What's Permissible to You

Go to what's permissible to you.

Search the book of laws.

Consider bypasses with the doctors.

Little loopholes are still reserved

For the rat the gecko and your age group.

A woman's photo exposes itself to you

And in your eyes cements Medusa's gaze.

A little drop of ice-cold water trickles down

The shoulder of a perky girl as she gets out of the pool,

A sweet world inside a crystal.

A molecule of innocence.

The white corpse of a poem lays upon a pale sidewalk

In front of an elementary school. That poem

Is you. The children trample all over you. But

In your earpiece still resound the pleasing sounds

Enslaved to your ear like hourly

Serfs.

So go to what's permissible to you.

To the doctors.

Ask for bypasses for your heart.

You are now permitted to do so.

Anyhow, on the crossing of three roads

Your son awaits to kill you.

It's what's permissible to him.

Walking with Myself

I walk next to myself

In silence.

I have harsh things to say to myself,

Very harsh even,

Blunt things.

But I won't say them here,

In the open air,

Where I might hear.

But nor in my sealed room

Will I say them

When I and myself shouldn't be with me.

A Thought

When a thought plummets at my feet

Bruised

I bandage its wings

Which I clipped

Until it revisits me

In faltering

Flight.

I then shoot it again.

The Worst of All

The worst of all passes me by
Like an actor memorizing
A long-forgotten role I go back
Learning my entire life by heart
As to not embarrass myself when I introduce
Myself to me

The worst of all passes
Me by
As if it were aiming for someone
Else.
It will notice
Its mistake.
And come back

Kamikaze

Under my bed I hoard

A collection of fears

To feed my nightly terrors.

And on horror-arid nights I

Scare myself

Like an old-fashioned locomotive stoker

That if the coal runs out he picks himself up

With his shovel and hurls into the fire

To make the train speed forward

And crash into the station.

A Small Light in the Corridor

Leave a small light in the corridor for the dead

Lest they forget that darkness must be feared,

And to allay the parting with the illusion of their life,

That they may foolishly believe we're still

In the next room, that they may call us

Mutely de profundis, and we shall come

To chase away the darkness that surrounds us, and extract

Them from their drawers like colored pencils

From a first-grader's desk drawer,

And illustrate a tender horror fairytale about themselves

And in limbo wander with them in a leaky refugee ship

Wedged between sealed ports that closed a gate before us

While another gate opened as night has fallen and soon

Dawn will rise above them like a strict den mother at a nursery

Waking, with rigid softness, those still asleep

Pleading to wait a slumber

For the resurrection of the dead.

A Feast

At every feast, at every banquet of perfumed

Embraces and orgies of raping gazes,

The shiny murderers sit with us at the table –

A hatchet knife for the fish, a saw knife for the meats, clanking

Chalices blinding. All destined to be sharply drawn,

Crashed, stabbed, spilled over the still

Rugs frightened witnesses to retribution acts by gangster

Families. The knife and the neck are separated solely by the calculated

Suspicious stare of loving relatives, as well as the hosts' tender

Soothing words like boxing referees forcing apart the fiery

Rivals to cool them down only to send them back to their

Deaths upon the ring.

Are you here to sacrifice or slaughter? The muted greeters ask

In every garden venue as they send you over to the hors d'oeuvre

Rings to which you stampede along with the rest of the rippers

And the ripped.

I offer a Compromise

> For my father, a beacon of enlightenment and tolerance. In eternal longing.

I offer a compromise.

I shall grind myself so thinly

that nothing but the dry wood remains

until I shall be so shiny

that the sun will be blinded by my sight

and perforate through me

your paper bodies.

I offer a compromise.

I shall stand in empty meeting rooms

as an exclamation mark

until the right spirits will fill in

the right chairs until papers be

exchanged either signed or flied

as long as peace will penetrate

the crazy bones of this house

and lend relief to those entering its

gates that gape upon them with a

yelp and close on them with a gulp

like a crocodile before he rests

in peace

I offer a compromise

I stop a cab and offer to the driver

I buy a paper and offer to the seller

I walk my dog and offer to his needs

I come to the shrink and offer to my complexes

I shall compromise and compromise until the compromise

will be thinly ground, until flour, until dust

which I shall bake to face bread

and to eyes bread

and to smiles bread

and peace shall descend on my gates

and tranquility in my bones

munched in the dogs' kennels

and relieve the crocodile that

swallowed me

with the sun

and a digestive

TO MYTH AND PLACES IN LUXURIOUS URNS

The Myth of Sisyphus
To Prof. Nurit Yaari. Se filia.

You mention Sisyphus, and I don't think about the curse,

And that guy pushing a rock up the mountain or

Its desperate decline but on the other one

Lying at the foot of the mountain, crushed to death

Under the tumbling rock.

At that moment, as Camus tells us, Sisyphus

Gains his biggest victory looking

Down, at all the distance he had come, basking in

His achievement even the Gods couldn't

Take away from him, blinded by the sight of the man lying

There, who in the meantime was joined by numerous crushed bodies

(Perhaps the shepherd from Cithaeron who quit his myth

In search of a lost sheep, or perhaps Dido

And Aeneas fornicating in some shadowy nook, perhaps

Someone who's heard of the man or of the punishment and the rock

And stopped by to peep and sneer).

The pile keeps getting higher, the rock's tumbling span

Keeps getting shorter. The Victory is getting smaller.

But Sisyphus and his rock will continue

To stand on top and brag,

Even when the pile of corpses covers the entire mountain

Burying them alive.

Oedipus Goes into Exile

The frenzied doves are pecking at the eyes of the morning
Knocking over the dishes given as provisions for his trip
To Colonos.
The door closes behind him like the eye of a dying cyclops.
He muddles along in a warm puddle of sunny gonorrhea
And to find his road of no return he
Scatters the pebbles of the doves' cadavers
Trampled by his sandals
Which he cannot see

Idomeneus

In the manner of Agamemnon and Jephthah of Gilead
Idomeneus the Crete only set out to Troy to sacrifice
The first one to step out of his home as he returns
Triumphant. Meaning, his son.
For the glory, the gore and the vengeance,
And for
One line in the mythos.

And truth be told, it wasn't the face
Which launched a thousand ships on an absurd, groundless
suicide mission
but
The prospect of holding a soft lock of hair
Paying no heed to the pleading cries
Sensing the faint breath exhaled
With gushes of blood spewing out of the delicate
Beloved
Mouth.
Your own flesh and blood.
To sleep no more.
To be forever cursed.
And to earn one line in the mythos.

A Literary Scholar Vacations in Corinth

To Yossi Yzraely. My mentor.

The inspired winds of Corinth wreak havoc on his hair, whitewashed

Like Medea's house, sealed shut but for the slaughter chamber

Which Jason rents out as a bungalow for classic Greek literature

Scholars.

The pamphlet offers a vegan menu of

Sun seeds and an entertaining computer game for the kids:

A ride to the sun and back in luxurious

Urns.

The city Interlaces

The city interlaces the black tresses of its avenues

Delicately anoints the lips of its horizon with crimson hues

Perfumes the labyrinth of its gardens' nudes

Much like Medea, preparing to slaughter her precious youths.

Walpurgisnacht

To my partners - Shimon, Sharon, Goethe and Else Lasker-Schüler

Sitting on a tattered straw lazy-boy

On a Tel-Aviv rooftop.

An Aztec goddess.

Ex.

The visa has expired.

So have the breasts.

She howls to the moon

Tries to ravage

Says wait for the eclipse.

Just you wait.

The little virgin girls' hearts

She ripped out in the kindergarten across the street

She dips in amchoor.

Her ancient back is chiselled

With harpoon

Calligraphy.

Angular. Thorny.

It's been ages since a man tried to decipher it.

The arches of her rheumatic fingers

Are commands for torching

Beheading, impaling, and demolishing

Hidden channels.

The neighbors summon investigators

To analyse.

They gather on adjacent rooftops.

A safe distance.

They sing along her Sumerian hymns.

Tell jokes in Acadian.

And from the cavernous bosoms of those little girls

Barbie princesses burst out. Galloping

On a pumpkin

For Walpurgisnacht.

Times Square: Heatwave Noon

Put on your flip-flops.

The sky is broken. You'll get hurt.

The kid doesn't get broken

Metaphors. He'll get hurt.

The cut will get infected. He

Will turn into a guru on the Fifth.

Or into a handicap.

Whichever comes first.

Meanwhile celestial angels

Are trampled on with earthly boots

Trying to pick up the pieces

Amidst the throngs of feet with their cups

To go to go to go, go on go on

In the square of times. The boss won't wait.

Nor will the king of beasts

Splattered on a sky scraper

Blinding those who walk in great

Auroras, dissolving the throne

Of the king of kings about

To crash on their heads

While dangling with his last bit of strength

In silent screams and a menacing

Poker face

On a hand atop

Times Square.

And now at the MoMA: a festival

Of Buster Keaton and silent

Films.

Venice

To Luca, Cristina, Giorgio, and the entire VIU gang. Salute!

Like the corpse in Rembrandt's Anatomy Lesson it lies

with open veins, her heart's blood flows turbid in the canals, and

the winged looks of her lovers dart upon her painted carcass with

the passion of physicians who forgot their patient in an

open heart surgery.

The narrowing alleys besiege them with the dark and wicked cholesterol

of hundreds of years of leprous stone

informers veil themselves with mask

on mask

CHAIN OF INFECTION

The Golem

The wind tiptoes inside

To caress our mourn-feigning faces

Like a compassionate and cruel doctor examining

Infectious plague victims

Molding in his bare hands the grace

Of their death and his own while still alive

And in the corner, his son sculpts the clay

Creating new humans.

Chain of Infection

When did the epidemic start in my head?

As soon as I said: from now on I shall write simple poems.

As soon as I divorced myself from the metaphor.

But she sneaks inside my bed every night

And titillates me.

As soon as I said: from now on I shall write by hand.

Not the computer. With Roland Barthes' pencil

That instantly erases everything you write. While you write.

And not on paper.

On your bare skin.

And when did the epidemic invade me.

As soon as I ripped out the window

And took in the spectacular view

Like a diseased, dishonored refugee,

Then gift-wrapped the ocean's horizon to his head

As a present to myself.

And he infected me.

And when did I die in the epidemic?

As soon as I tore off the buttons from my shirt

And flaunted my loins,

Saddled the Ashtoreth on it and galloped

To beget a new religion.

And she took away my breath

And left me a barren soil

Able to grow nothing but thorns

And politicians.

And I gathered myself to be gathered

To my forefathers. Sheaf by sheaf.

Now that everything closed down

Now that everything closed down,
That vain display windows
Withdraw inward and whisper
Like traitors:
You could have dispensed with us long ago.
Now that stages expose their misshapen
Backs, that tablecloths are pulled off
Tables in luxury restaurants
Like a seductive brassiere from the prosthetic
Silicon breasts of a top stripper,
Now that the belly is sucked in to silence
The bellows of the fattened ox,
Now that credit cards are converted to
Fortunetellers' cards calculating
Galactic Cataclysms,
And all the accountants
Consider how much more they can subtract
From their heavy clients so that they may
Elevate in the refracted light
Ascend upon the shaky rectitude
Of the spirit toward
The shells.
Toward themselves.

Notes from the House of Corona

Faint breaths of air blow my way from nature's

Unreliable ventilator. A sun as pale as a nurse plunging

Onto the horizon after twelve

Hours without a moment's rest

Infuses drops of light from a depleting

IV bag allocated to me from my dead neighbor who whistled

His happy 's' when he sprayed me with viruses.

*

As I write these lines my hands

Covered in white rubber gloves resemble

The noble dead of Thomas Mann

In Death in Venice strikes again

For which they are now broadcasting a promo.

Live.

*

I've decided to permanently discard of my body

A virus–ridden surface salivating poems

Known for being plagued with invisible

Viruses on the connotation level.

Entrance Strategy

When the hush before a concert is thrust
By the tyrannical conductor alert to every breath
I am as wary of my digestive system
As a sonar to a spy submarine.

The duplicitous snitch of my entrails' song
Keeps sending notifications. The ailment emergency depots
Are opened. There is plenty of stock. They properly prepared.

I have never so often washed my hands of washing my hands
of.
They're starting to cleanse the water.
All trials are postponed.

I mean it when I say that I love you.
The quarantine prevents me from providing character
witnesses.
Take me on probation. Be my probation
Officer. Only take me on now
When the sentence precedes the verdict
And guard and prisoner are to be incarcerated
In one cell until the white rubber glove
test, right-left,
Separates them.

WHAT'S IN A POEM?

Abandon all hope, ye who made it here.

The Unforgettable Line

I sometimes fancy I'm an unforgettable line

In someone's autobiography but

The light always circumvents me

Like a run-over cat.

We circumvent each other as reluctant

Acquaintances at the therapist's door.

Making light gestures of I

Don't exist and you never saw me. In fact, that's all

What the gnat inside Titus' head had said:

Pardon, I hate to interrupt your work,

But the exit sign is off, yes, that's

Where the temple is, no, I have no matches,

It's awfully dark in here, you never saw me, I

Don't exist, how do I get out of here, the light circumvents

Me, burn something so we see something.

What's the point of making history?

A run-over cat.

I sometimes fancy I'm an unforgettable line

In someone's autobiography

Like a rare disease.

With a magical tropical name.

And incurable.

The Poet's Fatigue

I plead my immense fatigue to subdue

Me like the dragon beseeching Saint George

To grow from his fertilized defeated body a kingdom on the banks

Of the Lethe River and graceful oblivion models will trot alongside it

Adorning a wreath of witless smiles.

Diagnosing Muse

No longer will any muse consent

To kiss him.

Not even on his brow.

Not even as a paid

Escort.

Today the poetry violates him

Like arthritis art

hritis

And he stands in the corner

And whimpers.

The Course of Poetry

Poetry begins suddenly

like a desperate fight for the life of a clinically dead.

Suddenly they stop torturing him with electric shocks

and astounding images

straight into the naked heart

the gaping feelings

the exposed breast

in front of the curious neighbours.

Poetry recommences suddenly

when they gather with laborious hush the torture instruments

like small children gathering twigs for an Auto-da-fé

then erupts a wondrous symphony of gathering the tools

and arranging the limbs under the sheet

and the sawing of a subdued whimper

and the crescendo closing of the ambulance doors.

And then poetry tides when swarms

of poets emerge from their holes

sharpen their canine tooth

wound with the spears of their nails

the asphalt of the orphaned road

and lick from the pool of blood

a feast for many a poem

Coming and Going

And after abandoning him poetry was back

As is the habit of women

Who forget only to return and return to

Abandon and gather in great haste,

Ignoring him ad disintegration, all they had obliterated

As is the habit of women: clotted menstruation, lifeless fetuses

Of beauty, starved gaping vulva lips, penmanship

Covering its shame, an open window overlooking the magnificent view

Of a suicidal thought, and a light toxic whiff

Of love from the gas burner she seemingly forgot to turn off

Only to abandon and return and clasp to her wilting bosom

The longing for his body as the beautiful fetus

Of her death

Cranes

> To Moti Lerner, freedom fighter

My thoughts are cranes

Migrating with the sedge in a spectacular pattern

In blind obedience no independent thought

In the winter to the warm south

North in the summer.

No independent thought.

Only when one gets lost

In thought, in its own poem,

And shot,

It finds its way.

Diving free and high

On joy

To crash upon the body of the hunter

Hurrying to save it.

Like Walter Benjamin

For Freddie

Like a lute
Touched by a breath of air
And it sings on its own
Wrote Walter Benjamin.

Like a breath of air
Touched by a lute
And it sings on its own
I write.

Like people
Bereft of air
Strangled by strings
Who touch themselves.

Like those
Who are no more.
And they touch us.
And we sing.

Like Walter Benjamin.

To my Kindred Poets:
To Bertolt Brecht. With thanks.

On days such as these

If I am to write a poem:

It's only under the condition that I can

Swap places with the condemned

The noose already round my neck

That's about to be broken,

And I am to declare my final wish.

Which is —

My poem.

The One and Only

The thread by which my life hangs.

A Brook

Yet truly I ask nothing more of

my life

But that it flows beside me rather

Than disturb my slumber. Calm

And grumbling it shall gaily

gurgle

Like the pure water of a brook

in a Japanese paradise

Perfect and

Breath–

Taking

ABOUT ATMOSPHERE PRESS

Atmosphere Press is an independent, full-service publisher for excellent books in all genres and for all audiences. Learn more about what we do at atmospherepress.com.

We encourage you to check out some of Atmosphere's latest releases, which are available at Amazon.com and via order from your local bookstore:

Blue, poetry by Gülru Gözaçan

Spindrift, poetry by Laurence W. Thomas

A Glorious Poetric Rage, poetry by Elmo Shade

Numbered Like the Psalms, poetry by Catharine Phillips

Verses of Draught, poetry by Gregory Paul Broadbent

Grafting, poetry by Amy Lundquist

How to Hypnotize a Lobster, poetry by Kristin Rose Jutras

Love Is Blood, Love Is Fabric, poetry by Mary De La Fuente

The Mercer Stands Burning, poetry by John Pietard

Lovely Dregs, poetry by Richard Sipe

Meraki, poetry by Tobi-Hope Jieun Park

Calls for Help, poetry by Greg T. Miraglia

Out of the Dark, poetry by William Guest

Lost in the Greenwood, poetry by Ellen Roberts Young

Blessed Arrangement, poetry by Larry Levy

Shadow Truths, poetry by V. Rendina

A Synonym For Home, poetry by Kimberly Jarchow

Big Man Small Europe, poetry by Tristan Niskanen

The Cry of Being Born, poetry by Carol Mariano

Lucid_Malware.zip, poetry by Dylan Sonderman

In the Cloakroom of Proper Musings, poetry by Kristina Moriconi

It's Not About You, poetry by Daniel Casey

The Unordering of Days, poetry by Jessica Palmer

ABOUT THE AUTHOR

Gad Kaynar-Kissinger was born in Tel Aviv (1947) and lives there. He is a retired Associate Professor from the Theater Department, Tel Aviv University, and the Chairman of the Israeli Writers Association. Kaynar-Kissinger is a stage, TV and film actor, a director, a former dramaturg of Israel's National Theater "Habima", the "Cameri Theater" of Tel Aviv, the "Khan Theater" of Jerusalem, and a co-editor of TEATRON, Israel's major theater magazine. He is a translator of 70 plays from English, German, Norwegian and Swedish into Hebrew. For his Ibsen translations he was appointed in 2009 "Knight First Class of the Royal Norwegian Order of Merit."

Kaynar-Kissinger's poems have been published widely since the late 1970s in major Israeli literary periodicals and supplements, and compiled in 8 volumes in Hebrew (the last ones being: *In the Heavenly Baby-Blue Nursery*, 2015; *Selfie* 2018; *High Risk* 2020). Kaynar-Kissinger's oeuvre also includes the bilingual Hebrew-Spanish publication *Lo que queda* (*What Remains*). For *ADHD* he won "The General Israeli Writers' Union" Award (2010).

Kaynar-Kissinger's poems have been translated and published in Spanish, Portuguese, Greek, Arabic and German. His English translations were published by *Pidgeonholes, Allpoetry, Anomaly Literary Journal, Atlas & Alice, The Bitter Oleander, Lady Blue Literary Arts Journal, Bombay Review, Reality Break Press, LOULIT, Indolent Books,* and others.

Gad Kaynar-Kissinger is married to the actress and speech coach Ahuva Kaynar. The couple has three children and eight grandchildren.